ENDORSEMENTS

"In our homeschooling curriculum, we have integrated Maureen Mink's series of books into our science lessons, connecting with nature through outdoor activities and understanding the spirit of animals. These books, and the lessons they inspire us to create, are helping my children gain a sense of global citizenship and environmental responsibility.

Maureen's captivating storytelling leads readers on a magical journey through the Navajo language and culture, leaving them enchanted by its beauty and knowledge. Enjoy the adventure!"

— **Jeanette Lee,** Mrs. Sweden World 2022,
High School English Teacher

"I wholeheartedly recommend 'Navajo Girl' by Maureen Mink. It's a captivating children's book that takes readers on an enchanting journey into the Navajo culture. The beautiful illustrations and engaging storytelling make it a must-read for both kids and parents."

— **Melissa Torres,**
Special Education Paraprofessional.

"The illustrations in Maureen Mink's book are absolutely eye catching and beautiful, capturing the richness of Navajo culture. It is also fun learning some words in Navajo language with the pronunciation guide allowing the reader to truly understand the importance of learning and connecting to the spirit of this book."

— **Jacquelyn Thomas,**
Best-Selling author of *'The Busy Bee'*

Maureen's books allow the reader to explore another culture while reminding us how all living things are equally precious. My son and I enjoyed learning some new words as well. Bravo Maureen...what a great, important series for us all to read.

— Scott Feld,
Best-Selling Children's author of *'Dax to the Max'*

"Maureen Mink's 'Navajo Auntie' and 'Navajo Uncle' will truly become the best part of your children's bedtime routine. It sparks meaningful conversations about the author's message of respecting all forms of life and our interconnectedness with nature. The illustrations are beautiful, and learning words in the incredible Navajo language is an added bonus!"

— Judy O'Beirn,
President of Hasmark Publishing International

NAVAJO AUNTIE

By Maureen Mink
Illustrated by Nino Aptsiauri

Published by:
Hasmark Publishing
www.hasmarkpublishing.com

Copyright © 2023 Maureen's Clans

First Edition

No part of this book may be reproduced or transmitted in any form or by any means, electronic or mechanical, including photocopying, recording or by any information storage and retrieval system, without written permission from the author, except for the inclusion of brief quotations in a review.

Disclaimer:

This book is designed to provide information and motivation to our readers. It is sold with the understanding that the publisher is not engaged to render any type of psychological, legal, or any other kind of professional advice. The content of each article is the sole expression and opinion of its author, and not necessarily that of the publisher. No warranties or guarantees are expressed or implied by the publisher's choice to include any of the content in this volume. Neither the publisher nor the individual author(s) shall be liable for any physical, psychological, emotional, financial, or commercial damages, including, but not limited to, special, incidental, consequential or other damages. Our views and rights are the same: You are responsible for your own choices, actions, and results.

Permission should be addressed in writing to ms.utahglobe2013@icloud.com

Editor: Jamie Geidel (Jamie.geidel@gmail.com)

Book Layout: Amit Dey (amit@hasmarkpublishing.com)

Illustrator: Nino Aptsiauri (artninka@gmail.com)

ISBN 13: 978-1-77482-225-8
ISBN 10: 1774822253

DEDICATION

In Navajo culture, we are one with all things. The land, animals, and humans all have equal value and are all respected as part of Mother Nature's incredible creations. This message of mutual respect and appreciation for all forms of life is the legacy that the author Maureen Mink hopes to share with her grandchildren, and with many more children all over the world.

This is a book that teaches children about the value of the natural world and the importance of preserving it, as well as connecting with and caring for the spirit of all things.

Yá'át'ééh, this book is dedicated to my grandchildren Wolf, Willow and my future grandchildren to come. To my husband Heriberto my love.

Our children Justine, Preston, Jaylynn, Yennika and Yadiel. To my siblings Melissa, Madeline and Darel. My nieces and nephews, Hannah, Brave, Navani, Eddie, Mia, Ava, Tea', Addie, and Brennen. To my mom and dad. To all the children everywhere that grow up to celebrate their stories and dreams.

Hózhó Náhásdlíí'.

This eagle in Navajo is Atsá (Ut-saw).
We can share them.

This bear in Navajo is Shash (Shuush).
We can share them.

This horse in Navajo is Łį́į́' (Klee')
We can share them.

This Antelope in Navajo is Jádí. (Jaa-Dee).
We can share them.

This tea in Navajo is Dééh. (De') it is used for tea and dye. We can share them.

This snake in Navajo is
Na'ashǫ́'ii (Nah-a show-ee).
We can share them.

This fish in Navajo is Łóóʼ (Klo)
We can share them.

This Dog in Navajo is Łééchąą'i (Kle'chan-a).
We can share them.

This skunk in Navajo is Gólízhii (Go-li-zhee).
We can share them.

This land in Navajo is Kéyah (Kee-ya).
We can share her too.

ABOUT THE AUTHOR

Maureen's paternal grandfather's clan is Tabaaha (Water's Edge), her father's clan is Tsénahabitnii (Sleeping Rock People) , and her mother's is Bilagáana (English/Irish). Maureen has a love for beauty in all things, which, in Navajo, is Hózhó. Maureen graduated from a pre-med program with a Bachelor of Science degree in Anthropology from the University of Utah, which brings her love of culture, beauty, and science together. Maureen's greatest joy and accomplishment is her family, and she wrote this book with them in mind. She wanted to leave a piece of her grandparents culture with them—and now all of you. She hopes you enjoy it.

CHECK OUT BOOKS 1 & 2 IN THE SERIES!

In Navajo culture, we are one with all things. The land, animals, and humans all have equal value and are all respected as part of Mother Nature's incredible creations. This message of mutual respect and appreciation for all forms of life is the legacy that author Maureen Mink hopes to share with her grandchildren, and with many more children all over the world. This is a book that teaches children about the value of the natural world and the importance of preserving it, as well as connecting with and caring for the spirit of all things.

In Navajo culture, we are one with all things. The land, animals, and humans all have equal value and are all respected as part of Mother Nature's incredible creations. This message of mutual respect and appreciation for all forms of life is the legacy that author Maureen Mink hopes to share with her grandchildren, and with many more children all over the world. This is a book that teaches children about the value of the natural world and the importance of preserving it, as well as connecting with and caring for the spirit of all things.

AVAILABLE ON AMAZON.

Giving a Voice to Creativity!

From: Circe'

To: Kids who love to write stories!

How would you like to have your story in a book? A real book! Hearts to be Heard will make that happen.

Get started now at
HeartstobeHeard.com

Also visit HH Kid's Corner for creative writing activities!
HeartstobeHeard.com/kids-corner/

PARENTS: Explore the possibilities for your child & others. Visit: HeartstobeHeard.com/parents

www.ingramcontent.com/pod-product-compliance
Lightning Source LLC
Chambersburg PA
CBRC091452160426
43209CB00023B/1874